Richard Hammond

Life's a Blast

First published in 2014 by Wayland

Copyright © Wayland 2014

Wayland
338 Euston Road
London
NW1 3BH

Wayland Australia
Level 17/207 Kent Street
Sydney NSW 2000

Senior editor: Julia Adams

Produced for Wayland by Dynamo
Written by Hettie Bingham

PICTURE ACKNOWLEDGEMENTS:
Key: b=bottom, t=top, r= right, l=left, m=middle,
bgd=background

Corbis: P17 br Martyn Goddard/Transtock. **Getty:** p2 tr,
p12 br AFP; p4 m, p6 tr, p12 mr, p16 mr, p18 ml, p24 br, p30 ml
Getty Images; p9 br, p29br Film Magic; p11 bl, p14 mr, p22 mr
Wire Image. **Rex Features:** p1 m, p5 tr, p16 bl, p20 mr, p20 br, p21 m,
p26 tr Christopher Jones. **Shutterstock:** Backgrounds and doodles:
smilewithjul; notkoo; LHF Graphics; hugolacasse; MisterElements;
Marie Nimrichterova; Aleksandr Bryliaev; Aleks Melnik; PinkPueblo;
mexrix; topform; P4 bm dea/a.de Gregorio; p5 bm bikeriderlondon; p5
br Balefire; p8 ml Marilyn Barbone; p8 m ET1972; p9 mt patjo; p15 tr
Ingrid Prats; p16 mr Bocman1973; p17 tl, p17 tr Bocman1973; p17 bl Faiz
Zaki; p19 m Ivan Cholakov; p20 bl BMCL; p23 mt Konjushenko Vladimir;
p23 tr Lasha; p23 mr sippakorn, p25 ml Balefire, p25 mr betto rodrigues.
Splash News: P15 bl Splash News. **iStock:** p7 tr sangfoto.

Dewey classification: 791.4'5'092-dc23

ISBN 978 0 7502 8260 4
E-book ISBN 978 0 7502 8561 2

Printed in China
10 9 8 7 6 5 4 3 2 1

Wayland is a division of Hachette Children's Books,
an Hachette UK company.
www.hachette.co.uk

The website addresses (URLs) included in this book were valid at the
time of going to press. However, because of the nature of the internet,
it is possible that some addresses or sites may have changed or closed
down, since publication. While the author and Publisher regret any
inconvenience this may cause, no responsibility for any such changes can
be accepted by either the author or the Publisher.

Richard Hammond

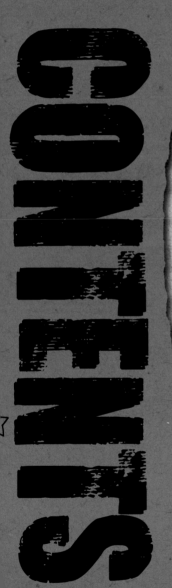

CONTENTS

RICHARD HAMMOND
The Hamster Himself!

■ Good things come in small packages…and Richard Hammond is a package that's exploding with energy and intelligence. Some know him as a petrol head and others think of him as a science boffin. Whichever way you see him, you'll probably agree that he's a fun guy with a great sense of adventure!

Life's a BLAST!

Richard loves to ride his bicycle through the city – even though his *Top Gear* pals tease him about it! He says it's the quickest way to beat the traffic. He's loved motorbikes and bicycles since he was a kid.

NAME: Richard Mark Hammond

NICKNAME: Hamster

BORN: 19 December 1969

HEIGHT: 1.70 metres (5ft 7inches)

FAMILY: Married to Amanda Etheridge (Mindy) with two daughters, Izzy and Willow

HOMETOWN: Solihull, West Midlands, England

RESIDENCES: Lives in a mock castle in Weston under Penyard, Herefordshire, England, and also has a flat in London

SCHOOLS: Solihull School and Ripon Grammar School

COLLEGE: Harrogate College of Art & Technology

OCCUPATION: Broadcaster, journalist, game show host and author

FAMOUS FOR: Presenting Blast Lab, Total Wipeout and Top Gear

LIKES: Science, playing bass guitar, cars, mock castles, cheese, animals and riding his bicycle

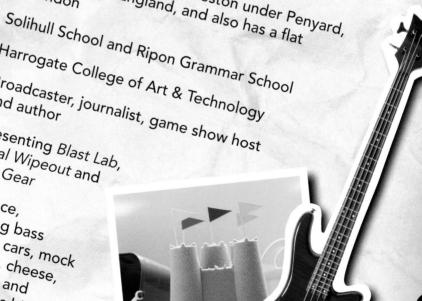

Little Richard

On 19 December 1969, Richard Mark Hammond was born.

DECEMBER 19

His early life was spent in Solihull in the West Midlands where he lived with his mother, Eileen, and father, Alan. He was soon joined by younger brothers, Andrew and Nicholas. There were just two years between each of the boys and they grew up as best friends. Richard once joked:

'I was always Batman ... they were the Joker and Robin!'

Richard is still as close to his brothers as ever.

Richard describes his childhood as happy. His obsession with wheels started with bicycles and then moved on to motorbikes and cars – he even had motorbike wallpaper.

When Richard was 11, he began to build his own bikes with his dad's help. His room used to be filled with boxes of spare parts to use for his projects. This was a hobby that continued until he was 15. Richard had longed for a motorbike since he was a small child and finally got one on his 16th birthday – a 49cc Honda.

RICHARD'S BEDROOM WAS FULL OF JUNK LIKE THIS ...

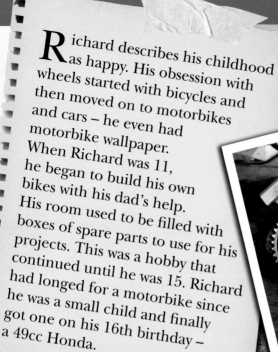

RICHARD'S EDUCATION

Richard began his education at Sharmans Cross School in Solihull. During the 1980s, Richard's family moved to Ripon in North Yorkshire, where he attended Ripon Grammar School. From 1987 until 1989, Richard went to Harrogate College of Art and Technology, where he obtained a National Diploma in Visual Communication.

Life's a BLAST!

Maybe it was because of his grandparents that Richard came to love cars so much; they worked in the Birmingham car industry, close to Solihull, where Richard spent his early years. Birmingham has a long history of manufacturing cars. Many thousands of people in the area worked for the automotive industry in its heyday. The Castle Bromwich assembly plant in Birmingham currently manufactures Jaguar cars.

Richard's Radio Days

When Richard left college in Harrogate, his first job was working at BBC Radio York as a programme assistant. Apart from making the tea, he got to drive around Yorkshire interviewing farmers. His stories dealt with trivial matters, such as vegetables that looked like something funny.

Richard's first radio interview was with a local organization, the Hammond Organ Appreciation Society. Sadly nobody ever got to hear it because Richard couldn't resist making lots of jokes about the Hammond name. His boss was clearly not impressed, as this first interview was never broadcast!

When Richard left BBC Radio York in 1990, he went to work at BBC Radio Leeds and then on to BBC Radio Newcastle. Next, he worked at Radio Cumbria where he presented *Lamb Bank* – a programme that puts farmers with orphaned lambs in touch with farmers who have ewes that have lost their young.

Finally, after stints at Radio Cleveland and Radio Lancashire, Richard left radio to follow his dream of presenting motoring programmes on TV.

'I LIKE TO THINK THAT I WAS A RATHER ROMANTIC FIGURE, A KIND OF WANDERING RADIO NOMAD – A BIT LIKE LASSIE WITHOUT THE BREATH AND TOILET HABITS.'

'RICHARD HAMMOND IS A GREAT TALENT AND A MUCH IN-DEMAND BROADCASTER. HE IS A WARM, FUNNY AND CLEVER BROADCASTER, WHO HAS NEVER LOST HIS RADIO ROOTS.'
LESLEY DOUGLASS, FORMER CONTROLLER OF BBC RADIO 2

Richard on Top Gear

In 1998, Richard Hammond was given his first motoring-themed job on television; he presented Motor Week on satellite channel Men & Motors. He also presented Car File for the same broadcaster. But it was only when Richard joined the Top Gear team that he seemed to find his true home on television.

Richard is awarded Best Presenter at t' EA British Academ' Children's Awards 2009.

Life's a BLAST!

Motoring has remained a keen interest of Richard's and in 2006 he appeared on Petrolhead, a BBC quiz show, as a team captain. Richard then presented a one-off documentary, Richard Hammond Meets Evel Knievel, in which he interviewed the motorbike stunt-rider shortly before his death in 2007.

Richard joined the *Top Gear* team in 2002 when the show was re-launched and broadcast from Dunsfold Aerodrome in Surrey. He has remained a part of the team ever since. Richard's *Top Gear* fellow presenters are responsible for giving him the nickname 'The Hamster' – inspired by his small size and his name. *Top Gear* holds the record for the world's most widely-watched factual TV programme.

The show has been broadcast in 212 different places around the world. When filming in the Ukraine, Richard couldn't get out of his hotel room because so many fans were outside.

In September 2006, Richard was seriously injured while driving a Vampire turbojet drag racing car for a feature on *Top Gear*. Although he was reaching speeds of up to 505 kilometres per hour (314mph), he made a full recovery. The show broadcast footage of the crash in 2007 and eight million viewers tuned in to watch (see page 12).

RICHARD SAYS:

'PEOPLE LIKE THE FACT THAT THERE'S AN ABSOLUTE HONESTY TO THE PROGRAMME. IF WE WEREN'T DOING TOP GEAR WE'D STILL BE OUT THERE BUYING CARS AND ARGUING ABOUT THEM. WHEN THE CAMERAS STOP ROLLING WE CARRY ON ARGUING - IT'S WHAT WE DO! ULTIMATELY, WE'RE THREE ORDINARY BLOKES WHO LOVE CARS.'

RICHARD HAMMOND ON PRESENTING TOP GEAR

When Richard went for an audition for *Top Gear*, he waited months before he heard anything back. He'd given up hope when they finally called him to give him the news that he'd been chosen. He told his wife: 'This will change everything.' And it did!

RICHARD'S ACCIDENT

Richard hit the headlines in 2006 when a stunt he was doing for a *Top Gear* show went badly wrong.

Travelling at around 463 kilometres per hour (288mph), he lost control of the jet-powered car he was driving. When the safety parachute failed to open, the car spun over several times.

> 'THERE WAS NO TIME TO FEEL REALLY FRIGHTENED ABOUT THE CRASH – I JUST THOUGHT IT WAS ALL OVER.'

The filming took place at a former RAF base in Elvington near York. Richard reached a top speed of 505 kilometres per hour (314mph) before he crashed. This was faster than the standing record, but was not recorded because it was never intended to be official. The plan was that he would drive as fast as he could and then explain how it had felt. But when one of the right front tyres blew, Richard lost control of the car.

> 'AFTER THE ACCIDENT I HAD A MEMORY SPAN OF ABOUT TWENTY SECONDS AT FIRST – SO AT LEAST I WAS EASY TO ENTERTAIN!'

An investigation was carried out to find out what had happened. This is what it had to say:

THE HEALTH & SAFETY
REPORT

'Richard Hammond's reaction to the tyre blow-out seems to have been that of a competent high-performance car driver, namely to brake the car and to try to steer into the skid. Immediately afterwards he also seems to have followed his training and to have pulled back on the main parachute release lever, thus shutting down the jet engine and also closing the jet and afterburner fuel levers. The main parachute did not have time to deploy before the car ran off the runway.'

Life's a BLAST!

When Richard regained consciousness after his accident, he thought he was in a hotel at a party. He kept asking his wife if they could go outside and have a drink. It took him a couple of weeks to accept that he had been in a crash and that he was in hospital.

RECOVERY

The Yorkshire Air Ambulance Service took Richard to the Head Injuries unit of the Leeds Infirmary where he was treated for a severe head injury. After a short time in a coma, Richard came round. He didn't have any visible injuries, but he found he had great difficulty remembering anything new.

Just four months after the accident, Richard was well enough to return to *Top Gear*. His team mates made a big fuss of him. Everyone was relieved and delighted to see him safely back.

THE VAMPIRE

The vehicle Richard was driving was a jet-propelled car called the Vampire. In theory, it was capable of up to 595 kilometres per hour (370mph). The Vampire still holds the Outright British Land Speed Record of 483.3 kilometers per hour (300.3mph) when it was set by Colin Fallows on 5 July 2000 at RAF Elvington.

WEIGHT: 998 kilograms (2,200lbs)

LENGTH: 9.14 metres (30ft) long

FUEL: Consumed 20-28 litres of fuel per kilometre (7-10 gallons per mile)

SPEED: It could accelerate from 0 to 438 kilometres per hour (272mph) in six seconds.

ENGINE: Rolls Royce Orpheus jet engine

Richard ON THE BOX

Although motoring is a firm favourite, Richard has presented shows on many others themes:

Brainiac

Brainiac: Science Abuse was a programme broadcast on Sky One between 2003 and 2008. The show featured bizarre experiments which set out to discover whether commonly held ideas are actually true. In one show, a swimming pool was filled with custard to prove that you could walk on it. A main feature of the show was the many explosions that were carried out in the name of science – but mostly just for fun!

Total Wipeout

From 2009 to 2012, Richard also presented Total Wipeout, a game show which took place in pools of water and mud. Contestants had to take part in a crazy assault course with the aim of completing it in the shortest amount of time.

Life's a BLAST!

Richard has also presented Crufts Dog Show, The 5 O'Clock Show, School's Out, Last Man Standing, Helicopter Heroes, Timewatch and Sport Relief.

Hamster's Wheel Productions

Richard owns a television production company, Hamster's Wheel Productions. He has joked that people warned him not to have a company name that has an apostrophe in it:

> And they were right; I've never seen it written properly. But there you go.

he commented. In conjunction with September Films, Hamster's Wheel Productions made the kids programme Blast Lab. It appeared on CBBC from 2009 until 2011. Characters called Ninja Nan and the Lab Rats helped Richard to present the show.

Blast Lab featured two teams of three kids: the Red Team and the Yellow Team. The teams were challenged to compete in wacky science games and perform explosive experiments. Topics included rocket propulsion, weight of liquids, magnetism, air pressure and gravity. Richard always found an interesting way to look at these subjects, whether it was building a hovercraft or racing balloons.

As well as producing 50 episodes of *Blast Lab*, Hamster's Wheel Productions co-produced two series of *Engineering Connections* for BBC2 and National Geographic (see page 21).

The Hamster's Wheels

When asked once which car he would choose if he could have any car that had ever existed, Richard said he would like to own an original 1964 Ford Mustang 350 GT Shelby racer. He doesn't yet have one of those in his collection, but here are a few that he does have:

Oliver – otherwise known as a 1964 Opel Kadett

This is a car that Richard acquired while filming in Botswana for *Top Gear*. He and his team mates were setting out to become the first people to cross the Makgadikgadi salt flats (pronounced macgaddy gaddy) in cars. He fell in love with the little motor and couldn't bear to cut it up and customize it as his team mates had done with theirs.

Oliver was the same model as this car.

At one point, Richard risked a crocodile infested lake to pull Oliver out with a chain. 'He looked after me, I looked after him,' said Richard, talking about the adventure on his return. Richard brought the little car back to England with him and had him re-sprayed and fixed up.
Oliver has become a bit of a star in his own right, having appeared on *Richard Hammond's Blast Lab* and on a further episode of *Top Gear*. He has a personalized number plate: OLI V3R.

'I'M SIMPLE-MINDED. MOST OF THE MOTORS IN MY COLLECTION OF... BANGERS AND CLASSICS ARE STRAIGHTFORWARD MACHINES.'

1968 Ford Mustang 390 GT

Close to his dream car, this vehicle takes pride of place in Richard's collection. The Ford Mustang inspired a new class of automobile which became known as the 'pony car', perhaps because of its logo showing a galloping pony. These cars were known for being affordable, compact, stylish and sporty.

Porsche 928

Richard bought this sports GT car for everyday driving. It is said to have the power of a sports car combined with the comfort, equipment and luxury of a saloon car. He is a big fan of Porsches and once owned a 1982 Porsche 911 SC, and later a 2006 Porsche 911 Carrera S.

Kawasaki ZZR1400

At a top speed of 300 kilometres per hour (186mph), this is one of the world's fastest, most powerful motorcycles. The Japanese bike manufacturer put a limit on the bike's top speed, so it is actually capable of going even faster! 'You barely have to nudge the throttle to feel the back end squirming about,' says Richard.

Morgan AeroMax

Richard recently sold this 1930s-style car. It looks a little like the Batmobile and, with its 4.8-litre BMW V8 engine, it can reach 273 kilometres per hour (170mph). Richard's Aeromax was one of only 100 that were ever made. Only six of them had right-hand drive manual controls like his.

Richard's Wings

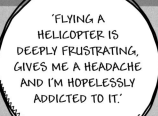

'FLYING A HELICOPTER IS DEEPLY FRUSTRATING, GIVES ME A HEADACHE AND I'M HOPELESSLY ADDICTED TO IT.'

It's not just wheels on tarmac that Richard loves to control. In 2010, he obtained his Private Pilot Licence flying a Robinson R44 helicopter.

To gain a Private Pilot Licence, Richard needed to successfully complete a course with a minimum of 45 hours of flight time. He had to pass seven written exams and also complete a solo cross-country flight. After having his flying skills tested by an examiner and taking an oral exam, he finally got his wings.

Richard has said that flying a helicopter is by far the most complicated thing he's ever learned. People have described flying a helicopter as being like patting your stomach and rubbing your head at the same time and Richard agrees that it is a bit like that.

Life's a BLAST!

Richard has his own Robinson R44. This is a four-seat light helicopter. It has one engine with a semi-rigid two-bladed main rotor, a two-bladed tail rotor and skid landing gear. The cabin is enclosed and has two rows of seating for a pilot and three passengers.

Flying a helicopter is a very technical process. The rotor blades create a force which makes the body of the helicopter want to turn in the opposite direction to the rotors. The pilot needs to push a rudder pedal to counterbalance that force. A lever makes the helicopter go higher but this makes the engine work harder so then you need to give the engine more power – there's a lot to think about all at once!

The strength of the wind can make a difference to how you need to use a helicopter's controls: sometimes the wind can be helpful and sometimes it can work against you, depending on its strength and direction. To fly a helicopter safely, you need to be concentrating and adjusting the controls all the time.

Richard the Tech-Head

Richard has always been fascinated by how things work. He is very interested in modern technology and how new advances shape the way we live today.

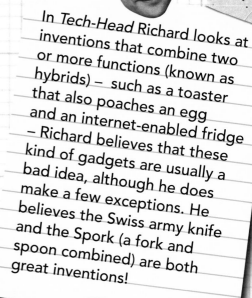

On his *YouTube* channel, *Richard Hammond's Tech-Head*, Richard likes to examine new technology. He points out that some of the best technology was invented during war time. For example, the first computer was invented to decode German messages during the Second World War in 1944.

In *Tech-Head* Richard looks at inventions that combine two or more functions (known as hybrids) – such as a toaster that also poaches an egg and an internet-enabled fridge – Richard believes that these kind of gadgets are usually a bad idea, although he does make a few exceptions. He believes the Swiss army knife and the Spork (a fork and spoon combined) are both great inventions!

'I COULD SEND AN EMAIL TO MY CHEESE.'

The Enigma decoding machine from World War II

Richard Hammond's Engineering Connections is a National Geographic series that looks at how engineers and designers use ideas from the natural world in clever ways to develop new buildings and machines.

Life's a BLAST!

As a child, Richard loved to experiment by building models out of everyday household objects. He once thought about following a career in engineering, but was actually offered a place at university to study architecture. Unfortunately, due to lack of funds, he was unable to take up the place.

'NATURE'S INFLUENCE ON ENGINEERING IS HUGE. WE'VE COME TO THE SAME CONCLUSION AS EVOLUTION – AND THAT'S HOW THE PROGRAMME WORKS,' EXPLAINs RICHARD. 'SOMETIMES WE'VE LOOKED AT NATURE TO SOLVE A PROBLEM. SOMETIMES WE'VE SOLVED A PROBLEM AND THEN REALIZED NATURE'S ALREADY DONE THAT.'

In the series, Richard does experiments and investigates some of the world's most incredible structures and inventions and discovers how they were engineered.

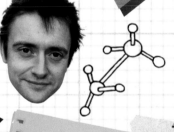

Richard is also interested in the future of motoring. He once commented:

We will find a means for storing hydrogen for fuel cells we could have an endless supply of fuel. That would make a big difference.

He is certain that we will still have cars in 100 years time. He recently said:

We will always want cars, no matter how digital, how clever the world is. We might not be travelling long distances because more people will be working from home. We might not want cars for boring practical reasons, but we'll do it for fun.

FAMILY LIFE

They say that an Englishman's home is his castle, but for Richard this is more than just an expression: he and his family actually live in a mock castle in Herefordshire.

Richard lives with his wife, Amanda Etheridge, who is known as Mindy. The couple met in 1995 and married on 4 May 2002, a day which Mindy has described as 'the best day of my life'. Mindy is a keen sportswoman; she loves tennis, running and swimming. Horse riding is her favourite activity and she has even managed to get Richard in the saddle. Richard and Mindy have two daughters named Izzy and Willow. As well as the many cars and bikes that sit on their driveway, Richard and his family own numerous animals. They have six dogs, four cats, eight horses, two goats, a flock of sheep, a peacock called Humperdinck, around twenty ducks and what Richard describes as 'an unnecessarily large collection of chickens'.

Richard with his wife, Mindy, and their two daughters, Izzy and Willow, at the UK premiere of *Madagascar: Escape 2 Africa* at the Empire Leicester Square in 2008.

After growing up as one of three brothers, Richard found it strange having daughters. 'When I had the girls a whole new world opened up,' he laughs, describing how the Land Rover is now 'full of hairbrushes and hockey sticks'.

Richards's eldest daughter, Izzy, loves to ride on the back of his motor bike. He has said that it was very brave of his parents to buy him a bike when he was 16 and that he will have to do the same for Izzy when she's old enough to ride one herself.

Richard's Family car is a Land Rover Defender 110 County Station Wagon. It is affectionately known as Wally Car, a name chosen by Richard's daughter Izzy when she was little. This is a vehicle that Richard has owned twice! Wally Car had been with the family on numerous holidays and even played a part in Richard and Mindy's wedding. Unfortunately, Richard had needed to sell it in 2001 and the family had been very sad to see it go. Then, one day when Richard took his daughter to play a netball match against another school, he found out that a teacher there had bought

Range Rover Defender 110

Wally Car all those years ago. He had been using it ever since to drive children around the world on various trips. Richard was delighted when the teacher agreed to sell it back to him. He put white ribbons on its bonnet, just like it had been decorated on his wedding day, and he surprised his wife by driving it home – as a gift for their wedding anniversary.

Charity Support

Like many celebrities, Richard gives something back to society by supporting certain charities. This is a great way to thank the public for their support and it shows he really cares.

Richard Hammond is a vice-president of UK children's brain injury charity, the Children's Trust. This is a leading charity for children who have suffered an injury that has caused brain damage. The Trust provides specialist care for children and young people from across the country. It also runs the UK's largest rehabilitation centre for children with brain damage, helping them to recover.

Richard and Amanda Hammond attend a dinner in aid of Women's Aid, 2007

In 2009, Richard appeared in the specially formed Top Gear Band in a performance for Comic Relief. He played bass guitar.

After Richard's accident in 2006, a charity appeal was launched in aid of the Yorkshire Air Ambulance, which had come to his rescue. At first, the money raised was going to be used for the day-to-day running costs of the helicopter. However, due to Richard's great popularity much more money was raised than anybody had expected, so the money was used to buy a second helicopter.

Richard supports Children in Need, a charity which provides support to thousands of youngsters aged 18 and under. The people the charity helps are affected by a wide range of problems, including homelessness and serious illnesses. As part of fundraising for Children in Need 2008, Richard appeared in a special episode of a TV drama called *Ashes to Ashes* in which he tried to test drive a car.

Richard has contributed to charity in a more personal way too. He recently helped to grant the wish of a little girl who was very ill by driving her around in a bright pink Lamborghini. This was part of a campaign by the charity Rays of Sunshine. The eight-year-old from Herefordshire had a serious lung condition and was confined to a wheelchair.

Richard has also helped to raise funds for Sport Relief. Money from this charity is used to help those in need in the UK and around the world.

20 FANTASTIC facts about RICHARD HAMMOND

RICHARD BUILT HIS OWN SPORTS CAR LIMO AND THEN DROVE THE POP SINGER JAMELIA TO THE BRIT AWARDS IN 2007.

RICHARD HAS NEVER WORKED AS A PROFESSIONAL DRIVER.

IN 2008, RICHARD SWITCHED ON THE BLACKPOOL ILLUMINATIONS WITH HIS TOP GEAR TEAM MATES.

RICHARD HAD TO ABANDON HIS PORSCHE 911 DURING SOME BAD FLOODS IN JULY 2007; HE HAD BEEN STUCK IN TRAFFIC FOR THIRTEEN HOURS. HE RAN ALL THE WAY HOME SO THAT HE COULD SEE HIS DAUGHTER ON HER BIRTHDAY.

IN A BRYLCREEM POLL IN DECEMBER 2007, RICHARD WAS VOTED THE CELEBRITY WITH THE 'BEST HAIR ON TV'.

RICHARD WAS AWARDED 'TV PERSONALITY OF THE YEAR' AT THE GQ MEN OF THE YEAR AWARDS IN 2007.

WHEN RICHARD FIRST WOKE UP AFTER HIS ACCIDENT, HE WAS CONVINCED HIS WIFE WAS FRENCH.

RICHARD HAMMOND'S FAVOURITE DINNER IS COTTAGE PIE.

RICHARD WRITES ABOUT MOTORING IN A WEEKLY COLUMN FOR THE DAILY MIRROR.

ON AN EPISODE OF TOP GEAR, RICHARD WAS IN A CAR THAT WAS ARTIFICIALLY STRUCK BY LIGHTNING.

IN MARCH 2006, RICHARD PRESENTED THE BRITISH PARKING AWARDS AT THE DORCHESTER HOTEL IN LONDON. CATEGORIES INCLUDED 'PARKING TEAM OF THE YEAR' AND 'BEST NEW CAR PARK'.

WHEN RICHARD PRESENTED A PROGRAMME CALLED THE GUNPOWDER PLOT: EXPLODING THE LEGEND, HE REBUILT THE HOUSE OF LORDS AND BLEW IT UP AS GUY FAWKES HAD TRIED TO DO IN 1605.

RICHARD'S FAVOURITE TREAT IS CHERRY BAKEWELL TART.

RICHARD USED TO SING AND PLAY BASS IN A BAND WHEN HE WAS YOUNGER. HE CAN PLAY THE DOUBLE BASS TOO.

RICHARD IS CO-INVENTOR OF THE GAME FANTASY CAR GARAGE WITH TOP GEAR CO-HOST JAMES MAY.

ONCE ON TOP GEAR, AFTER AN ARGUMENT WITH JEREMY CLARKSON ABOUT WHICH CAR WOULD GO ON THE 'COOL WALL', RICHARD ATE THE CARDBOARD PICTURE OF THE CAR HE LIKED, LIVING UP TO HIS NICKNAME OF 'HAMSTER'.

RICHARD WAS ONCE HYPNOTIZED ON TOP GEAR CAUSING HIM TO FORGET HOW TO DRIVE A CAR.

WHEN RICHARD WAS 5 YEARS OLD, HIS DAD HELPED HIM WORK OUT HOW MANY DAYS THERE WERE UNTIL HE COULD DRIVE A CAR.

WHEN RICHARD FIRST HEARD THE NEWS HE WAS GOING TO BE A TOP GEAR PRESENTER, HE WAS SO HAPPY HE CRIED.

WHEN THERE ARE NO REAL CARS CLOSE AT HAND, RICHARD LIKES TO PLAY WITH REMOTE-CONTROLLED CARS.

ARE YOU BEST MATES WITH...

RICHARD HAMMOND?

By now you should know lots of things about Richard. Test your knowledge of him by answering these questions:

1 What was Richard's first ever motorbike?
a) A 49cc Honda
b) A BMW HP2 Sport
c) A Yamaha MT-01

2 In which town did Richard spend his first years?
a) Windsor
b) Solihull
c) Edinburgh

3 Richard's career began in Radio, but for which station?
a) BBC Radio Leeds
b) BBC Radio Cleveland
c) BBC Radio York

4 In which year did Richard first join the Top Gear team?
a) 2002
b) 1998
c) 1980

5 How tall is Richard?
a) 1 metre
b) 2.2 metres
c) 1.7 metres

6 What is Richard's middle name?
a) Nigel
b) Mark
c) Archibald

7 In which industry did Richard's granddad work?
a) The car industry
b) The space technology industry
c) Show business

8 In which TV show did Richard fill a swimming pool with custard?
   a) Blast Lab
   b) Top Gear
   c) Brainiac: Science Abuse

9 What is the name of Richard's production company?
   a) Yucky Gucky Films
   b) Hamster's Wheel Productions
   c) Lazy, Crazy Productions

10 Richard has a pet Peacock – what is it called?
   a) Humperdinck
   b) Hugo
   c) Elvis

11 Which instrument did Richard play in the Top Gear Band?
   a) Harp
   b) Nose flute
   c) Bass guitar

12 What does Richard fly?
   a) Paper aeroplanes
   b) Pegasus
   c) A helicopter

ANSWERS

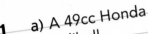

1 a) A 49cc Honda
2 b) Solihull
3 c) BBC Radio York
4 a) 2002
5 c) 1.7 metres
6 b) Mark
7 a) The car industry
8 c) Brainiac: Science Abuse
9 b) Hamster's Wheel Productions
10 a) Humperdinck
11 c) Bass guitar
12 c) A helicopter

Richard has written the following books:

On the Road: Growing Up in Eight Journeys – The Early Years (Orion, 2013)

Richard Hammond's Great Mysteries of the World (Random House, 2013)

On the Edge: My Story (Orion, 2008)

Richard Hammond's Blast Lab (Dorling Kindersley, 2011)

Car Science (Dorling Kindersley, 2011)

Can You Feel the Force?: Putting the Fizz Back into Physics (Dorling Kindersley, 2010)

Or is That Just Me? (Orion, 2009)

You can find more information about Richard Hammond by:

Logging onto the *Top Gear* website at www.topgear.com or following him on Twitter @RichardHammond.

Quote sources

Page 6 *The Guardian*, 2013; **Page 9** www.bbc.co.uk; **Page 11** *Friday Night with Jonathan Ross*, 2009; **Page 12** *Friday Night with Jonathan Ross*, 2007; **Page 15** www.thehamstercage.co.uk; **Page 16** *The Daily Mirror*, 2009; **Page 18** www.topgear.com/uk/richard-hammond/richard-hammond-helicopter-2009-01-06; **Page 20** *Richard Hammond's Tech Head*, YouTube; **Page 21** *Richard Hammond's Tech Head*, YouTube; **Page 22** www.thehamstercage.co.uk; **Page 23** *Friday Night with Jonathan Ross*, 2009.

GLOSSARY

Architecture
Planning, designing and constructing buildings

Assembly plant
A factory where parts of machines are put together

Audition
To try for a performing role

Automotive industry
A term that covers a range of companies involved in manufacturing and selling cars

Boffin
An informal word for a scientist or engineer

Counterbalance
A weight that acts to balance out another weight

Customize
To alter an item to a personal specification

Engineering
The use of scientific knowledge to design and build structures

Footage
Material that has been filmed or recorded by movie or video cameras

Guy Fawkes
A man who attempted to blow up the houses of parliament in 1605

Hammond Organ
An electric organ invented by Laurens Hammond and John M. Hanert in 1935

Heydey
A period in the life of a person or activity when it is at its peak of strength and popularity.

Hypnotize
To send someone into a trance

Lassie
A fictional collie dog made popular by the novel Lassie Come Home and a series of adventure films.

Logo
A graphic design used to market and identify a product

Nomad
A person who does not stay in the same place for a long time

Oral Exam
An exam that is spoken rather than written.

Rotor blades
The four rotating blades of a helicopter

Trivial A matter of little importance

INDEX